The
Essential
Flipbook *for*
Achieving
Rigor

1400 Centrepark Blvd., Ste. 1000
West Palm Beach, FL 33401
717.845.6300
email: pub@learningsciences.com
learningsciences.com

Printed in the United States of America

22 21 20 19 18   1 2 3 4 5

Publisher's Cataloging-in-Publication Data
provided by Five Rainbows Cataloging Services

Names: Dujon, Amy, author.
Title: The essential flipbook for achieving rigor / Amy Dujon.
Description: West Palm Beach, FL : Learning Sciences, 2018. | Series: Essentials series.
Identifiers: LCCN 2018941910 | ISBN 978-1-943920-52-5 (pbk.)
Subjects: LCSH: Teaching–Methodology. | Effective teaching. | Education–Aims and objectives. | Learning strategies. | Classroom environment. | BISAC: EDUCATION / Teaching Methods & Materials / General. | EDUCATION / Professional Development.
Classification: LCC LB1025.3 .D85 2018 (print) | DDC 371.102–dc23.

The Authors

This Flipbook would not be possible without the hours of research, years of experience, and unceasing drive for school improvement each author brought with them to the *Essentials for Achieving Rigor* series. Thank you to all our authors.

Gwendolyn L. Bryant

Jennifer A. Cleary

Libby H. Garst

Laurine Halter

Kelly Harmon

Elizabeth Kennedy

Kathy Marx

Robert J. Marzano

Carla Moore

Terry A. Morgan

Tracy L. Ocasio

Amber C. Rutherford

Tzeporaw Sahadeo-Turner

Ria A. Schmidt

Connie Scoles West

Penny L. Sell

Deana Senn

Edited by Amy M. Dujon

Introduction

This flipbook of classroom tips and techniques for the **Essentials for Achieving Rigor Instructional Model** has been designed to provide classroom teachers with an overview of the key criteria, plus multiple sample techniques, for each of the elements in the Essentials model. To use this book effectively, you should have at least an introductory understanding of the Essentials model's planning and teaching strategies, and have already begun to use the model in your standards-based classroom to increase rigor in student learning.

In a standards-based classroom, students are expected to meet a defined standard for proficiency. The primary purpose of the Essentials model is to help teachers develop the expertise to teach rigorous lessons with both the creativity (the art) and the research-based knowledge (the science) needed to ensure success for all students. The key criteria and sample techniques in this book will help you intentionally plan to implement research-based classroom strategies to take your rigorous instruction to the next level.

we have organized this book according to the components on the teaching map illustrated on the next page to include the three elements in **Criteria for Success**, the 13 **Instructional** elements, and the five **Conditions for Learning**.

As you plan to use each technique in your lessons, first review the key criteria to understand the big picture of the element. For example, if you are planning to use the strategy "Helping Students Process Content" in a lesson, you'll note that one of the *key criteria* includes grouping students to encourage discussion and interaction. When you turn to the *techniques* page, you will find four sample strategies to use with students working in groups to process content: jigsaw, reciprocal teaching, concept attainment, and paraphrasing. You are encouraged to use these sample techniques as a jumping off point to research or design your own techniques for each element.

For a deeper dive into each of the components and elements in the Essentials Model, see the **Essentials for Achieving Rigor Series** of books published by Learning Sciences International.

STANDARDS-BASED CLASSROOM
TEACHING MAP

LSI MARZANO CENTER
ESSENTIALS
FOR ACHIEVING RIGOR

Standards-Based Planning

Criteria for Success
- Providing Rigorous Learning Targets and Performance Scales
- Using Formative Assessment to Track Student Progress
- Celebrating Student Progress

MONITORING FOR LEARNING WITH STUDENT EVIDENCE

Instruction
- Identifying Critical Content
- Previewing New Content
- Organizing Students to Interact with Content
- Helping Students Process Content
- Helping Students Elaborate on Content
- Helping Students Record and Represent Knowledge
- Managing Response Rates with Question Sequence Techniques
- Reviewing Content
- Helping Students Practice Skills, Strategies, and Processes
- Helping Students Examine Similarities and Differences
- Helping Students Examine Their Reasoning
- Helping Students Revise Knowledge
- Helping Students Engage in Cognitively Complex Tasks

MONITORING THE LEARNING ENVIRONMENT

Conditions
- Establishing Rules and Procedures
- Recognizing Adherence and Lack of Adherence to Rules and Procedures
- Using Engagement Strategies when Students are Not Engaged
- Establishing and Maintaining Effective Relationships
- Communicating High Expectations for All Students

Using Formative Assessment Data for Instructional Decisions

Collaboration

The Learning Map for the Essentials for Achieving Rigor Model

Celebrating Student Progress

Providing Rigorous Learning Goals and Performance Scales

For students to reach mastery of rigorous standards, learning goals and targets must be established and communicated. **Learning goals** are created from the essential skills and knowledge embedded in state approved academic standards and express what the student will know and be able to do. Depending on the type of knowledge required by the standard, the learning goal might be formatted using declarative knowledge (information and concepts), procedural knowledge (strategies, skills, or processes) or a combination of both. **Rigorous learning goals include high levels of both cognitive complexity and student autonomy.**

A distinction should be made between learning goals and learning activities or assignments. Activities and assignments are the means by which learning goals are accomplished; they should never be considered the learning goal themselves.

While goals focus on developing competence, performance scales explain the trajectory and learning progression the student needs to master to demonstrate proficiency or surpass the goal. The levels of the performance scale scaffold in cognitive complexity. The learning goal, gleaned from and aligned with the cognitive complexity of the state or district standards, is placed at Level 3.0 on the performance scale. The learning goal is usually broken into instructional **learning targets** that address specific knowledge and skills students must understand to demonstrate the standard. The Level 2.0 on the performance scale consists of learning targets that include the foundational concepts required to build to the Level 3.0 learning goal. Level 2.0 targets are therefore at the level of cognitive complexity below the learning goal or standard. On the other hand, Level 4.0 targets are more complex than the learning goal at the Level 3.0 requiring the students reach above the level of complexity of the standard and what was taught.

Learning goals and performance scales provide direction and structure for classroom learning and should be referenced numerous times during a lesson. Both goals and scales require intentional planning. Monitoring techniques should be determined and intentionally planned to verify students understand the learning goal and what the scale means.

Providing Rigorous Learning Goals and Performance Scales

A technique to communicate rigorous learning goals and/or targets embedded in a performance scale must be utilized.

There are many different techniques that can be used for this purpose. *Techniques provided are a sample and should not be considered a comprehensive list.*

Technique	Description
Post It	Display the learning goals and performance scale in the classroom for the students to see.
Student- Friendly Language	Students work independently or in groups to create their own wording for each scale level and related learning targets after the teacher thoroughly explains the progression of learning from simple to complex.
Refer to It	Make reference to the learning targets, goal, and scale often during the lesson.
Share It	Distribute a written or electronic version of the learning targets, goal and performance scale to students and guardians.
Relate It	Relate classroom activities and assignments to the learning targets, goal, and scale throughout the lesson.

These and more techniques can be found in *Becoming a Reflective Teacher* by Robert J. Marzano (2012).

Using Formative Assessment to Track Student Progress

Both teachers and students should track progress toward the learning targets and goals. Teachers should track progress **to inform and adjust instruction** to meet the needs of the students. Students should track their own progress **to verify the status of their learning** in relation to the learning target **and determine how to close the gap** to reach the learning goal.

Students should be allowed some latitude in how they express what they understand and are able to do. Assessment formats and conditions can vary as long as all forms of the assessment measure the same learning targets.

Once students understand the learning goal, targets, and performance scale, they can be used to formatively access student academic progress. Anything that students do autonomously that is aligned to a learning target can be used as an assessment to track student progress.

Formative assessments are used during instruction to determine what the students did or did not learn and what they can or cannot do.

Formative assessments to track student progress require intentional planning. Monitoring techniques should be determined and intentionally planned to verify **students understand their current status on the scale and can articulate their progress toward the learning goal.**

Using Formative Assessment to Track Student Progress

A technique to formatively assess and track student progress must be utilized to determine whether students understand their current status on the scale and can articulate their progress toward the learning goal.

There are many different techniques that can be used for this purpose. *Techniques provided are a sample and should not be considered a comprehensive list.*

Technique	Description
Proof of Achievement (POA)	A short focus problem or exercise provided to students to demonstrate progress and verify achievement of 2.0, 3.0, or 4.0 level targets on the scale.
How Did It Help?	Students self-assess their status and progress toward the learning goal by explaining how what they did in class helped them achieve the learning target.
Rate Yourself Exit Card	Students write on an index card the level of performance they achieved providing justification for their rating.
Level Up	Students identify learning targets achieved and determine what they need to do to move to the next level on the scale.
Student-Generated Assessments	Student-created tasks that demonstrate knowledge of the learning target(s) and their current status toward the goal. Students use this demonstration of knowledge to move from one level on the scale to the next.
Chart Progress	Students record their progress toward the learning goal over time using a chart or some other tracking method.

These and more techniques can be found in *Becoming a Reflective Teacher* by Robert J. Marzano (2012).

Celebrating Student Progress

One of the most powerful aspects of formative assessment is that it allows students to see their progress over time. Knowledge gain should be recognized and celebrated to motivate students to continue progress toward the goal.

Both students' individual knowledge gain and current or final score on the scale should be celebrated. Acknowledgement can be made collectively or discretely. It is important to remember that the recognition and celebration must always be **tied to the learning** that takes place related to the Criteria for Success (learning goal, targets, and performance scale).

Celebrating student progress requires intentional planning. Monitoring techniques should be determined and intentionally planned to ensure **students feel pride in their knowledge gain and accomplishments and are motivated to continue progress toward the goal.**

Celebrating Student Progress

TECHNIQUES

A technique to celebrate student progress must be utilized to ensure students feel pride in their knowledge gain and accomplishments and are motivated to continue progress toward the goal.

There are many different techniques that can be used for this purpose. *Techniques provided are a sample and should not be considered a comprehensive list.*

Public

Technique	Description
Knowledge Gain Celebration	The growth or difference between the initial and current score for a learning goal or target is determined, and students are recognized by the amount of growth or knowledge gain achieved over a period of time. Gains of any amount should be acknowledged and celebrated.
Final Status Celebration	At the end of the unit or completion of the learning goal students are recognized by the scale level achieved. For example, all students who reached the 3.0 level are asked to stand for a round of applause or their names are displayed on a poster in the room. Students that reached the 3.5 and 4.0 levels are recognized in a similar manner.
Celebratory Messages Home	Individual student progress is shared with parents or guardians through text messages, phone calls, or notes home acknowledging knowledge gain or final status.

Private

Technique	Description
Verbal Feedback	Specific feedback is provided to students explaining what they did well in their learning. Comments should relate to learning goal progress and may include phrases concerning work ethic, focus, effort, preparation, well-structured, challenge, etc.
Written Feedback	Notes are written on assessments, student journal, etc. to acknowledge knowledge gain toward learning targets or final status.

These and more techniques can be found in *Becoming a Reflective Teacher* by Robert J. Marzano (2012).

Instructional Strategies

Identifying Critical Content

Before every lesson a few key points should be identified that are essential (critical) for students to achieve mastery of the content and the learning target. To identify the critical content for a lesson, unpack the standard to determine what students should **know** and **be able to do**. This critical content becomes the learning targets for the lesson.

Critical content should be identified and presented using a clear progression that guides students to deeper understanding of the content, goal, and standard.

These points should be emphasized numerous times and in a variety of ways during instruction. Not everything presented or discussed is critical and students must be able to discern what is and is not important.

Identifying critical content requires intentional planning. Determine how to introduce and identify the critical content and guide students through that progression of content.

Monitoring techniques should be determined and intentionally planned to **verify students know what content is important and what is not important.**

Identifying Critical Content

Techniques used to identify critical content should help students determine what presented content is important and what is not important. Critical content should be presented using a clear progression to lead students to a deeper understanding of the content and standard.

There are many different techniques that can be used for this purpose. *Techniques provided are a sample and should not be considered a comprehensive list.*

Technique	Description
Visual Cueing	Storyboards, graphic organizers, pictures, videos, demonstrations, interactive websites, illustrations, works of art, illustrated PowerPoint slides, etc. are used to highlight the critical content and help create mental images for the content being taught.
Storytelling	Narrative stories are used to help anchor critical content into memory and signal that certain information is important.
Dramatic Instruction	Involves students in dramatizing the content through re-enactments, role-plays, skits, dramatic readings, hand gestures, movement, and dance to encourage an emotional connection with the content and signal the importance of the material being presented.
Verbal Cueing	Critical content is verbally cued by directly stating the important information, raising and lowering the voice, and pausing at key points during the presentation. Verbal cueing signals the importance of the content and gives students time to think about the content presented.
Advance Organizers	A linguistic or nonlinguistic technique to cue critical content and assist students in identifying and organizing their thoughts around what is important and what is not. Organizers can be designed to give students the big picture, build connections to the past and for the future, or could be a metaphor to help organize teaching and learning.

These and more techniques can be found in *Identifying Critical Content: Classroom Techniques to Help Students Know What is Important* by Deana Senn, Amber C. Rutherford and Robert J. Marzano (2014) and *Becoming a Reflective Teacher* by Robert J. Marzano (2012).

Previewing New Content

Previewing helps students activate prior knowledge relative to the new content. Students pull from life experiences and previous learning to make links between new content and what they already know. Previewing activities should build curiosity about the new content and encourage discourse among students. They should be short, engaging, and fun activities that make obvious links and provide proof of knowledge.

Previewing New Content requires intentional planning to activate students' thinking. Determine how to guide them to make links between their prior or related knowledge and the new content they are about to learn.

Monitoring techniques should be used to **verify students have successfully linked what they know to what is about to be learned.**

Previewing New Content

KWL/RAN Chart

- KWL—A chart that includes columns for K (What I know), W (What I want to know), and L (What I learned). Students complete the first two columns before the lesson then complete the last column after lesson completion.

- RAN—"Reading and Analyzing Nonfiction" chart is a modification of the KWL chart. The RAN chart usually has five columns: Prior Knowledge (What I think I know), Confirmed (Yes, I was right), New Learning (What I learned), Misconceptions (What I couldn't prove) and Wonderings (What I still want to know). The last three columns can be combined into one if desired. Students place sticky notes in the first column stating what they think they know on a topic before they read the text. They read the text and then move the sticky notes that are confirmed to the second column. Students are then asked to move any incorrect notes or misconceptions to the misconception column and add new sticky notes for new information or "wonderings."

Anticipation Guide

- A short survey that includes a series of True/False statements about the upcoming content. Students revisit the guide after the content has been taught to review their knowledge gain and clarify misconceptions.

A previewing technique is the method used to help students activate prior or related knowledge and make connections to the new content about to be learned.

There are many different techniques that could be used to preview new content. *Techniques provided are a sample and should not be considered a comprehensive list.*

Skimming

- Written information on upcoming content is scanned to determine main ideas and important concepts. Students summarize their understanding of what they read, record how well they already understand the content, and predict what they will learn during the lesson or upcoming unit.

Brief Teacher Summary

- Oral or written synopsis describing highlights of upcoming content used by students to anticipate key ideas and patterns during content presentation.

Preview Questions

- Questions asked to peak curiosity, activate prior knowledge, and signal what information students should be looking for as new content is presented.

These and more techniques can be found in *Becoming a Reflective Teacher* by Robert J. Marzano (2012).

Organizing Students to Interact with Content

KEY CRITERIA

Organizing students to interact with content helps students **learn, deepen, and enhance their understanding** of the content. Students benefit from the multiple perspectives experienced during group interaction. Interacting in groups allows students to see how others process the content and see how others react to their processing of the content.

Organizing students to interact with content is often used in conjunction with other strategies or techniques (e.g., students are grouped to review content, grouped to process critical content, grouped to examine similarities and differences, etc.). When the learning target includes mastery of skills or processes, give students time to practice independently before grouping them with other students.

The purpose for the grouping and activity must be made explicit to the students for meaningful interaction to occur. **Establish, explain, and model rules for conduct and routines for interaction.**

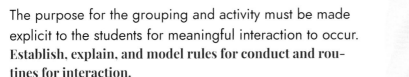

Groups of two to five students work best. Larger group sizes often erode individual accountability.

Learning groups can be *heterogeneous* (mixed ability) or *homogeneous* (same ability) in nature. If the purpose of the grouping is to help struggling students, heterogeneous groups work best. If the purpose of grouping is to encourage medium or average ability students to learn at high levels, then homogeneous groups work best.

Organizing Students to Interact with Content

The techniques used to organize students to interact with content should assist their learning and enhancing of the content. The purpose of the grouping, the number of students in the group, the roles and responsibilities of the members, and accountability methods should be determined before organizing the students for the activity.

There are many different techniques that can be used for this purpose. *Techniques provided are a sample and should not be considered a comprehensive list.*

Pair Grouping

Technique	Description
Think-Pair-Share	Students think about a presented problem or question independently at first, then form partners to share thoughts, ideas, and possible solutions to the problem or question. After coming to consensus the pair shares what they decided with the class.
Think-Pair-Square	An adaptation of the think-pair-share technique. Instead of sharing with the class at the end, the pair confers with another pair to share and discuss solutions, thoughts, or approaches.

Organized Grouping

Technique	Description
Round Robin	Students are arranged in a circle in groups of four. Group members listen as one student leads off the process by offering his/her opinion, thought, reaction, or idea to a posed question. When finished, the student sitting to the left responds and the process continues moving clockwise until everyone has made a contribution. The session concludes with a group discussion.
Placemats	Using the diagram shown, students brainstorm and write their thoughts about a topic in their respective outside space. A round robin is then conducted for each person to share his/her thoughts. Common views or points are noted in the center circle. Each group then shares the common points they discussed with the entire class.

Structured Grouping

Technique	Description
Perspective Analysis	Students identify their point of view on a given topic and determine their reasoning behind their outlook. They identify opposing viewpoints and the reasoning behind it, then summarize what they have learned by analyzing both perspectives.
Thinking Hats	Students examine an issue from six different points of view exploring one perspective at a time. A different color hat symbolizes each mode of thinking. • **Blue hat** represents organization and manages the thinking process and the other hats. • **White hat** represents the neutral perspective and presents the information and facts at hand. • **Red hat** represents emotional perspective and relies on intuition, gut instinct, and feelings about the topic. • **Black hat** represents the cautious perspective and identifies reasons to be careful and conservative. • **Yellow hat** represents optimistic perspective and identifies benefits and valuable aspects of an idea. • **Green hat** represents creative perspective and generates new ideas and offers novel solutions.

These and more techniques can be found in *Organizing Students to Interact with Content: Classroom Techniques to Help Students Know What is Important* by Deana Senn and Robert J. Marzano (2014) and *Coaching Classroom Instruction* by Robert J. Marzano and Julia A. Simms (2013).

Helping Students Process Content

A shift from a teacher-centered classroom to a student-centered classroom **is required to help students process and generate conclusions** about the content. Students should discuss, summarize, associate, predict, and clarify the content as they are learning, not just be passive listeners.

In order to help students process, content should be chunked and instruction should stop at strategic points. Questioning and student evidence should be used to help determine the appropriate size of the content chunk.

Group students to encourage the discussion and interaction needed to help them process content. Roles should be assigned when students are asked to process content in groups.

Helping Students
Process Content

TECHNIQUES

A processing technique is the method used to help students **summarize, predict,** and **clear confusions** about the content.

There are many different techniques that could be used to help students process content. *Techniques provided are a sample and should not be considered a comprehensive list.*

Technique	Description
Jigsaw	Students are grouped together into teams. Each student on the team is assigned a segment of the content or topic to learn. The base team disbands and students meet with their "expert" groups to discuss and learn the assigned content or topic. Students return to the base team to teach assigned content and learn remaining content from other base team members. Questions should not only ask to summarize the content, but to assist with predicting and clarifying misconceptions.
Reciprocal Teaching	Before new content is presented, members of a small group generate predictions about the upcoming content chunk. After the content is presented, one student acts as discussion leader facilitating the discussion and asking questions about the content. After all questions have been addressed another team member summarizes the content and the group makes predictions about the upcoming content to be presented. The role of discussion leader is rotated and the discussion of the next chunk of content continues. Another method is to assign roles like "Predictor", "Summarizer", "Clarifier", and "Questioner" and rotate roles with each new chunk of content.

Concept Attainment	A structured inquiry process where students compare and contrast examples and non-examples to identify attributes of a concept. Since the "content objective" is not provided, the students hypothesize about the attributes of the concept. To demonstrate that they have "attained" the concept, students think of other examples and non-examples to validate their thinking.
Paraphrasing	Students reflect on what is said (or read) and restate both the words and the feelings of the speaker (or author) to clarify the content presented. Information is condensed and restated in different words, not repeated. New ideas are not introduced nor are questions asked during the paraphrasing process.

These and more techniques can be found in *Becoming a Reflective Teacher* by Robert J. Marzano (2012)

Helping Students
Elaborate on Content

KEY CRITERIA

To help students elaborate on the content, they should be asked **questions that go beyond what was taught**; questions that require them to make inferences about what else might be true. Students should also be asked to explain or justify their reasoning by providing evidence and support for their inferences.

Elaborative questions should be planned prior to instruction and interspersed throughout the lesson. Questions should scaffold in complexity and wait time must be provided to allow students to think about the content and make the necessary links to infer and elaborate.

Student autonomy is cultivated if students are required to answer all questions. In other words, the question should never be answered by the person asking the question. Instead the questioning technique should be adjusted to provide the scaffolding necessary to support the students' thinking and help them connect with the question.

Helping Students Elaborate
on Content

There are two basic questioning techniques to help students elaborate on content. They involve two general categories of questions. Responses to questions can be verbal, written (linguistic or nonlinguistic) or demonstrated in some other manner.

General Inferential Questions

- Questions that require students to generate inferences about content or make connections between existing background knowledge and content to predict, make informed decisions, or draw conclusions.
    - Default questions
        - Require students to make inferences using their background knowledge to determine an answer
    - Reasoned inferences
        - Require students to construct an answer based on logical thought and speculation of the content presented

Elaborative Interrogations

- Questions that extend reasoned inference by requiring students to provide logical support and evidence for their conclusion.
    - To help students provide evidence to support conclusions ask "How do you know/why do you believe that to be true?"
    - To help students make generalizations about categories of persons, places, things or events ask "What are some characteristics or behaviors you would expect of...?"
    - To help students make if/then generalizations about the content ask "What would you expect to happen if...?"

Helping Students Record
and Represent Knowledge

Students should record or represent their understanding of content and processes **in their own words**. When recording, students should jot down words or phrases that represent key ideas. Students can also represent the knowledge gained nonlinguistically using symbols, movement, or pictures. Types of representation should include mental models, mathematical models, and other more abstract representations of content.

Recording and representing knowledge should be used as students are learning new content. These records or representations should then be revisited once understanding of content deepens in order to revise and reflect on any changes in understanding of knowledge. Students should not be asked to record and represent knowledge during direct instruction, but should be given time after each content chunk is presented and processed to record the critical content in their own words. A variety of note taking, recording, or representing formats should be introduced to the students so they can be encouraged to utilize the method they most prefer.

Helping Students Record and Represent Knowledge

Linguistic Representation

Generating Notes—students summarize critical content using their own words.

Types of Notes	
Combination Notes	Students use a two-column format to include both written notes and nonlinguistic representation to record thinking.
Informal Outlines	Students determine the most important information to include and use indentation to indicate the relative importance.
Free-Flowing Web	Students use connected circles and lines to form a web that represents connections between the concepts.

A recording and representing technique is the method used to help students **document, symbolize, encode,** and **express** the content.

There are many different techniques that could be used to help students record and represent knowledge. *Techniques provided are a sample and should not be considered a comprehensive list.*

Academic Notebooks—a record of students' analysis and synthesis of content that can include generating notes, reactions to content, questions, answers, and reflections.

Nonlinguistic Representation

Graphic Organizers—Students record their knowledge using a graphic that demonstrates relationships or represents patterns in the content.

Dramatic Enactment—Students role-play characters, scenes, processes, events, etc., or symbolize (act out) the content in some manner.

Mnemonic Devices—Rhymes, phrases, acronyms, and songs used to help students retain and recall information.

These and more techniques can be found in *Recording and Representing Knowledge: Classroom Techniques to Help Students Accurately Organize and Summarize Content* by Ria A. Schmidt and Robert J. Marzano (2014) and *Becoming a Reflective Teacher* by Robert J. Marzano (2012).

Managing Response Rates with Question Sequence Techniques

KEY CRITERIA

A questioning sequence based on the learning targets and goal should be planned and implemented to guide students through the thinking necessary to generate deep understanding of the content. All levels of cognitive complexity should be embraced in a question sequence. **A linear progression of questions** should be utilized that requires students to:

- articulate **details** about the content

- identify characteristics of content related **categories**

- **elaborate** on identified categories

- provide **evidence** and support for those elaborations

These four phases of the questioning sequence can **span multiple days or be conducted in one class period.** In some cases, students may need to seek information from outside resources and texts in order to answer questions posed.

The sequence of questions should be based on learning targets, in order to build purposefully in cognitive complexity toward the learning goal. Question sequencing is best when intentionally planned, but can also be used spontaneously any time the opportunity presents itself.

Managing response rates with question sequence techniques should be employed throughout the progression of learning to provide opportunities for multiple students to respond using critical thinking and active processing. Monitoring techniques should be determined to verify **students have an opportunity to respond to a sequence of questions that require them to critically think about the content.**

More information about using question sequence techniques can be found in *Questioning Sequences in the Classroom* by Robert J. Marzano and Julia A. Simms (2014).

Managing Response Rates with Question Sequence Techniques

Techniques to manage response rates provide the opportunity for students to think critically about the content as they reply to a sequence of questions. Techniques under this strategy fall into two categories: **individual student response** and **group response**.

There are many different techniques that could be used for this purpose. *Techniques provided are a sample and should not be considered a comprehensive list.*

Individual Student Response—Response techniques that are posed during whole-group discussions or activities that call on multiple students for each question give students a chance to rehearse their responses before being called on, ask students to defend their responses, call on students randomly, ask students to record their responses, or allow students to challenge each other's responses.

- **Response Chaining**

  - Students respond to each other's answers following four steps. (1) Teacher poses question; (2) Student A responds; (3) Teacher asks student B to identify student A's answer as correct, incorrect, or partially correct and explain why; (4) If student B incorrectly identifies student A's answer, the teacher can call on student C to respond to student B's response.

- **Paired Response**

  - Pairs confer and determine a response to the question. Teacher calls on the pair and one or both can contribute their answer.

- **Short Written Responses**

  - Students record their individual responses and throughout the lesson periodically compare their responses to specific questions.

Group Responses—Students collaborate in groups and respond collectively. These techniques are especially helpful when questions involve different perspectives or competing opinions and are valuable during the category, elaboration, and evidence phases of the questioning sequence.

- **Sticky-Note Brainstorming**

  – Students write any legitimate answer to the posed question on a sticky-note then post them to the board for the entire class to view. The class then fills in missing information and discusses which answers might not be valid responses.

- **Group Listing**

  – The class is divided into the same number of groups as there are questions. Each group receives a question and jointly come up with as many examples or answers as possible. The groups then rotate question and answer lists and add to the new question and set of answers. This process continues until the lists return to the original groups. The groups review their original answer lists and reorganize the information based on importance or relevance with the most important listed at the top and the least important at the bottom. The students share their final answer list with the class and explain why they ordered the items like they did.

- **Numbered Heads Together**

  – Students form small groups and number off in each group. The students compare answers to the posed question. The teacher then calls out a number and the student in each group assigned that number stands to answer the question. The teacher resolves any misconceptions before the students sit down and the process is repeated for the next question.

These and more techniques can be found in *Questioning Sequences in the Classroom* by Robert J. Marzano and Julia A Simms (2014).

Reviewing Content

Critical content should be reviewed to shape understanding and deepen learning. Brief, repeated exposure of previously taught content helps students identify basic relationships between ideas and consciously analyze how one idea relates to another. Review activities should be **fast, friendly and fun, with the students doing the reviewing,** not the teacher. The cumulative nature of the content should be highlighted throughout the review process.

Reviewing Content requires intentional planning. Determine how to guide the students to produce an accurate representation of previously taught critical content. Techniques should be established to monitor whether **students can successfully show what they learned as it relates to the critical content.**

Reviewing Content

TECHNIQUES

The technique used to review content should help students produce an accurate representation of previously taught critical content and should highlight the cumulative nature of the content.

There are many different techniques that could be used for this purpose. *Techniques provided are a sample and should not be considered a comprehensive list.*

Technique	Description
Cloze Activities	The teacher presents previously learned information to students with pieces missing and asks them to fill in the missing pieces.
Summaries	Students write or verbally share a quick summary of previously learned information, what they thought important, or what they remember.
Review Stations	Multiple areas of the room are designated as "stations" that involve reviewing different chunks of critical content or different review activities (summarizing, demonstrations, practicing). Students rotate through each station to complete the brief review.
Brief Practice Exercise	Students complete an exercise or problem that prompts them to remember and apply previously taught critical content.
Questioning	Questions are asked that require students to recall, recognize, or apply previously learned critical content. Questions might also ask students to make inferences or decisions based on previously learned information.

These and more techniques can be found in *Becoming a Reflective Teacher* by Robert J. Marzano (2012).

Helping Students Practice Skills, Strategies, and Processes

Practice activities help students develop fluency, automaticity, accuracy, speed, controlled processing, and alternative ways of executing procedures. Practice provides the think time required for students to deepen their understanding of the content instilling **confidence** and **competence** with the skill, strategy, or process.

Sessions should be guided and conducted when students initially work with the content. The skill, strategy, or process should be modeled and retaught as necessary to help students reach success. To move students toward independence, content should be scaffolded in complexity and sessions should become less structured the more they practice. Students should ultimately apply the appropriate skill, strategy, or process without prompting.

Helping students practice requires intentional planning to determine how to help students develop automaticity or controlled processing.

Techniques should be established to monitor whether students can successfully practice the skill, strategy, or process quickly, fluently, automatically, or with controlled processing.

Helping Students Practice Skills, Strategies, and Processes

TECHNIQUES

Guided Practice—Practice sessions designed to provide well-structured guidance and support to students as they gradually organize, review, rehearse, shape, summarize, compare, and contrast the skill, strategy, or procedure.

- **Close Check**

  - While students are learning a new skill, the teacher provides a highly structured environment and watches student actions very closely to correct early errors or misunderstandings.

- **Frequent Structured Practice**

  - During initial learning, the teacher begins the session with a demonstration of the skill or process followed by numerous structured opportunities to practice isolated elements of the skill or process. Support is provided to ensure a high probability of student success with the practiced skill or process. Students should experience success multiple times before moving away from this type of practice.

Independent Practice—Less structured practice sessions designed to involve increased cognitive complexity and self-directed, autonomous work from the student.

- **Varied Practice**

  - Students practice the skill in more thought-provoking situations. The students work harder because the cognitive complexity involved increases due to task challenges and obstacles. Students should be encouraged to think metacognitively and monitor their progress and

The technique used to help students practice should support students as they **develop automaticity or controlled processing** with skills, strategies, or processes by engaging in appropriate practice activities.

There are many different techniques that could be used for this purpose. *Techniques provided are a sample and should not be considered a comprehensive list.*

speed to identify their strengths and weaknesses in execution of the skill or process.

- **Fluency Practice**
  - Autonomous practice with a focus on performing or executing the skill, strategy, or process skillfully and accurately with either automatic or controlled processing. This type of practice is often assigned as homework.

These and more techniques can be found in *Becoming a Reflective Teacher* by Robert J. Marzano (2012).

Helping Students Examine Similarities and Differences

KEY CRITERIA

Examining similarities and differences helps students deepen their content knowledge by identifying basic relationships between ideas. **Comparison, classification, analogies, metaphors, and manipulating mental images** all help students strengthen understanding and forge new connections in their schema. Students should be asked to draw conclusions and summarize what they learn as they examine similarities and differences. Students should be asked to generate mental images and represent similarities and differences linguistically or nonlinguistically.

Helping students examine similarities and differences requires intentional planning. Determine how students will describe the similarities and differences between elements and share what new information they have learned as a result of their comparisons. Techniques should be established to monitor whether **students can summarize, represent, draw conclusions, and explain how examining similarities and differences deepened their understanding** of the content.

Helping Students Examine Similarities and Differences

The technique used to help students examine similarities and differences should support students as they **compare, classify, create analogies and metaphors, identify basic relationships between ideas, and generate or manipulate mental images.**

There are many different techniques that could be used for this purpose. *Techniques provided are a sample and should not be considered a comprehensive list.*

Sentence Stem Comparisons

- Sentence stems used to contrast various people, places, events, concepts, or processes and provide structure for students to follow when making comparisons. This structure guides students and helps maintain focus on the same feature or characteristic thereby avoiding common errors in thinking.

  _____ and _____ are similar because they both _____ _____ and _____ are different because_____

Comparison Matrix

- Chart used to make comparisons between two or more concepts or elements and their characteristics or attributes. Students summarize what they learned by comparing the elements.

Comparison Matrix				
Attributes to be Compared	Element 1	Element 2	Element 3	Similarities and Differences
Attribute 1				
Attribute 2				
Attribute 3				
Summary:				

Classification Chart

- Chart used to group or sort similar content into categories based on characteristics. Categories can be predetermined and items sorted by those categories or students can create their own categories based on their knowledge of the characteristics of the items involved.

Classification Chart		
Category 1	Category 2	Category 3

Similes or Metaphors

- Students state comparisons using "like" or "as" (similes) or as direct relationships (metaphors). Students should provide an explanation as to why their simile or metaphor is appropriate and accurately represents the content.

Analogies

- **Sentence Stem Analogies**

  – Stems are provided to create comparisons that describe specific relationships between two items or concepts. The usual form is "A is to B as C is to D because..." Students should provide an explanation for the created analogy that reflects their depth of understanding.

- **Visual Analogies**

  – A visual organizer is used to make analogies and specify the type of relationship being represented by the analogy.

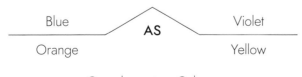

Complementary Colors

These and more techniques can be found in *Becoming a Reflective Teacher* by Robert J. Marzano (2012).

Helping Students Examine
Their Reasoning

Students should be asked to **produce and defend claims** as they examine their reasoning or the logic of presented information, processes, and procedures. They need to examine the strength of support presented, identify the reasoning behind it, and uncover errors in content or their own reasoning. Students should explore information to disclose informal fallacies. They should be asked to examine the logic behind procedural knowledge and determine more efficient ways to execute processes. Students should be encouraged to investigate the reasoning behind multiple perspectives. This strategy needs to be modeled for students and support must be provided as they learn to examine and defend reasoning.

Helping students examine their reasoning requires intentional planning. Determine how students can **identify and articulate errors in logic or reasoning, or the structure of an argument, and explain new insights resulting from their analysis.**

Techniques should be established to monitor whether students can support a claim, identify errors in reasoning, describe errors in content, explain the overall structure of a presented argument, and identify the reasoning behind multiple perspectives thereby deepening their understanding of the content.

Helping Students Examine Their Reasoning

TECHNIQUES

The techniques used to help students examine their reasoning should verify that students can **identify** and **articulate** errors in logic or reasoning, or the structure of an argument, and **explain new insights** resulting from this analysis.

There are many different techniques that could be used for this purpose. *Techniques provided are a sample and should not be considered a comprehensive list.*

Practicing Identifying Common Errors

- Practice exercises are created to help students identify common errors in logic or reasoning. Categories of errors are faulty logic, attacks, weak reference, and misinformation.

Categories of Errors in Reasoning	
Faulty Logic	Claims based on flawed reasoning that stems from contradiction, accident, false cause, begging the question, evading the issue, arguing from ignorance, and composition or division
Attacks	Claims that attack rather than logically supporting the claim (poisoning the well, arguing against the person, appealing to force)
Weak Reference	Claims based on ineffective sources like those that reflect bias, lack credibility, appeal to authority, appeal to the people, or appeal to emotion
Misinformation	Claims that confuse the facts or misapply a concept or generalization

Examining Support for Claims

- Students examine the support provided for a claim by analyzing the grounds (initial evidence), backing (additional information to establish validity), and qualifiers (exceptions to claims) that support it.

Statistical Limitations

- Errors that commonly occur are found and analyzed when using statistical data to support a claim. The five types of statistical limitations are: regression toward the mean, conjunction, base rates, the limits of extrapolation, and the cumulative nature of probabilistic events.

Examining Multiple Perspectives

- Similar to Perspective Analysis where students determine the reasoning behind multiple perspectives, identifying and analyzing opposing positions, and summarizing new insights gained from the analysis.

These and more techniques can be found in *Becoming a Reflective Teacher* by Robert J. Marzano (2012), and *A Handbook for the Art and Science of Teaching* by Robert J. Marzano and John L. Brown.

Helping Students
Revise Knowledge

Students should be asked to reexamine their understanding of the content by reviewing what they previously learned. **Multiple exposures** allow students to revise their knowledge by correcting errors or misconceptions and adding new information or insights gained to deepen their understanding of the content.

At this stage of instruction, accuracy of the content becomes paramount. In order for students to realize what they know (or don't know), they need opportunity to record or represent what they learn early in the instructional cycle. They should then be encouraged to **revisit earlier work and recordings to correct, clarify, and expound upon** their knowledge of the content. It is important that students not only revisit the facts, but be provided an opportunity to revise their thinking about the bigger ideas and connections within the content.

Helping students revise knowledge requires intentional planning. Determine how students can **examine previous knowledge** to correct errors or misconception as well as **add new insights** gained during the learning process. Have students explain how their understanding has transformed or examine how the current lesson changed their perceptions and understanding of previous content.

Techniques should be established to monitor whether students can make additions and deletions to previous knowledge that deepen(s) their understanding of the content.

Helping Students Revise Knowledge

The techniques used to help students revise knowledge should verify that students can **make additions and deletions to previous knowledge** that deepens their understanding.

There are many different techniques that could be used for this purpose. *Techniques listed are a sample and should not be considered a comprehensive list.*

Revising Notes

- Students are asked to make a new entry in their notebooks after a critical input experience, group work or processing, or after reviewing and correcting homework. Over the course of the unit and during related units, students reexamine their notebook entries to correct inaccuracies or incomplete information.

Academic Review

- Students review their completed activities, tasks, and notes to identify the important vocabulary terms, big ideas, concepts, generalizations, and understandings they should study for an exam or a quiz. This review of information is used to create study guides, review and revise thinking, or generate questions about the information.

Peer Feedback

- Students analyze their peer's notebook or completed task work according to teacher provided criteria, guidelines, or questions. Students might answer questions like the following:

  - What methods did the student use to express or represent information that was especially clear or concise (i.e., graphic organizers, flowcharts, summaries, pictures, etc.)?

  - What information was recorded that I did not record in my notes?

– What do I consider to be the most important information recorded?

– What is one thing the student could improve on when recording knowledge in his/her notebook or on the task sheet?

Assignment Revision

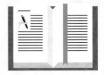

• Comments are made on student assignments, but scores are only recorded in the teacher gradebook not on the assignment. Students are offered an opportunity to revise the assignment and resubmit it to try to get a higher score. Students that do not resubmit a revised assignment accept the initial unknown score, but scores are adjusted for those that do resubmit based on the quality of revised work.

These and more techniques can be found in *Becoming a Reflective Teacher* by Robert J. Marzano (2012), and *A Handbook for the Art and Science of Teaching* by Robert J. Marzano and John L. Brown.

Helping Students Engage in Cognitively Complex Tasks

KEY CRITERIA

Once students have had the opportunity to learn, practice, and deepen their understanding of the content, the instructional cycle should culminate with **a thought experiment or a short or long term cognitively complex task.** Complex learning involves the students in reality-based, thought-provoking tasks connected to a learning target on the scale where a question or prompt stimulates further exploration of content. Students generate a hypothesis and predict what they will discover or conclude, then support or refute that prediction based on evidence. Generating and testing hypotheses moves the students beyond basic levels of knowing and requires experimentation with new knowledge.

Four key components are required to effectively implement an activity that engages students in cognitively complex tasks.

1. Students should **present and support claims.** Students should be aware that to be valid, claims need to be supported (grounds), the grounds need to be explained (backing), and exceptions to the claims should be identified (qualifiers) (*The Art and Science of Teaching* by Robert J. Marzano, 2007).

2. Students should **generate conclusions** and state why they think their claim is correct or not.

3. Students should **identify common logical errors** or exceptions to the rule that may limit their analysis and application of content.

4. Students should **navigate digital resources** to integrate various sources of information.

When helping students engage in complex tasks, the role of the teacher is to facilitate the learning, organize the students, and support them with the guidance and resources needed to predict, discover, conclude, defend or dispute a claim. Cooperative learning, peer response groups, or student-designed tasks could be used when organizing students for complex learning. To facilitate the learning and provide support, the teacher could examine student claims for errors, grounds, backing, and qualifiers or interview students to track progress on the task and provide feedback.

Helping students engage in cognitively complex tasks requires intentional planning. Determine how students can enhance their new knowledge by participating in authentic learning tasks. The task should have students generate conclusions, identify common logical errors, present and support claims, navigate digital resources, and identify how one idea relates to others.

Techniques should be established to monitor whether students enhance their new knowledge by engaging in cognitively complex and authentic learning tasks.

Helping Students Engage in Cognitively Complex Tasks

TECHNIQUES

The technique used to help students engage in cognitively complex tasks should confirm that students enhance their knowledge by requiring generation and testing of hypotheses and analysis of thinking.

Investigating

- When students use investigating to generate and test hypotheses, they use what others have said or written as opposed to observing the data themselves. To do this, students state a claim, then gather evidence to convince their audience that the claim is valid. Evidence that contradicts the initial claim is not discounted. The contradiction or confusion is acknowledged and can be used to support or refute the conclusion that students draw from their investigation. Students develop a plausible resolution and finally reflect on their initial claim. There are three types of investigations:

Types of Investigations	
Historical Investigations	Based on past events
Projective Investigations	Based on future or hypothetical events
Definitional Investigations	Describe characteristics of places, things, or concepts

There are many different techniques that could be used for this purpose. *Techniques provided are a sample and should not be considered a comprehensive list.*

Problem Solving

- When students use problem solving to generate and test hypotheses, they generate possible solutions to overcome an obstacle or constraint, and test and defend (or refute) their possible solution. Students analyze their own thinking as they test possible solutions using established criteria and defend their conclusions based on evidence they document during testing.

Decision Making

- When students use decision making to generate and test hypotheses, they predict a best choice among alternatives and analyze their thinking to judge those alternatives based on criteria to make an informed decision. Alternatives and criteria can be provided by the teacher or determined by the students.

Experimental Inquiry

- When students use experimental inquiry, they generate a hypothesis and collect evidence by direct observation to test their hypothesis. Students develop and implement a procedure for collecting the evidence. The teacher can provide a prompt, or narrow the topic or content by asking students to come up with their own prompts. One way a teacher can set up a prompt is to conduct a demonstration, or set up an observation for students that can then springboard into questions they want to find answers for.

These and more techniques can be found in *Engaging in Cognitively Complex Tasks: Classroom Techniques to Help Students Generate & Test Hypotheses Across Disciplines* by Deana Senn and Robert J. Marzano (coming 2015) and *Becoming a Reflective Teacher* by Robert J. Marzano (2012).

Conditions
for Learning

Establishing Rules and Procedures

Effective classroom management begins with establishing rules and procedures. **Rules identify general expectations and standards, whereas procedures communicate expectations for specific behavior** (Emmer et al., 2003).

The beginning of the school year or course is the most appropriate time to establish rules and procedures. Time should be spent making sure students understand the rules and procedures and they should be practiced enough for students to be able to execute them in a routine manner. Establishing rules and procedures is associated with a decrease in disruptive behaviors, and discussion of the rationale behind the rules and procedures breeds success. Interaction with students, periodic reviews, and classroom meetings may be required to modify and maintain the learning environment.

Another important factor to consider when establishing rules and procedures is the physical arrangement of the room. The classroom should be **organized for effective teaching and learning**. Physical conditions should be modified or created to facilitate and support ease of student movement and ready access to materials and technology.

Establishing Rules and Procedures

TECHNIQUES

Posting Rules

- Rules are posted in relevant locations. Group-work rules might be posted near the group-work space, rules for leaving the classroom might be posted by the door and rules for supplies, near the storage area.

Posters and Graphics

- Students create posters and graphics that emphasize the importance of specific rules and procedures or specific character traits important to proper classroom behavior.

Gestures and Symbols

- Gestures or symbols are used to communicate basic messages in the classroom. When a teacher raises his/her hand, it might signal the need for attention. Blinking the lights might signal that group work has become too noisy. Pointing to the list of rules might signal students to stop and consider their behavior at that moment. Students raising their pencil might indicate help is needed from the teacher.

Reviewing Rules and Procedures

- If students seem to systematically disregard the rules and procedures, the lapse is discussed and suggestions are requested to help correct the behavior. The rule might be redesigned, suspended, or dropped after the review.

These and more techniques can be found in *Becoming a Reflective Teacher* by Robert J. Marzano (2012).

The technique used to establish rules and procedures should confirm that students know classroom rules and procedures, can move easily about the classroom, and have easy access to materials.

There are many different techniques that could be used for this purpose. *Techniques provided are a sample and should not be considered a comprehensive list.*

Recognizing Adherance and Lack of Adherance to Rules and Procedures

A balance of positive reinforcement and negative consequences for adherence and lack of adherence to rules and procedures should be established for effective learning to take place. This system of acknowledgement and consequences should be communicated at the beginning of the school year or course and addressed frequently and consistently throughout the year.

Students who follow the rules and procedures and provide a positive influence to the class culture should be recognized. Equally, students who misbehave and detract or interrupt the learning environment should also be identified. **Rules and procedures for which there are no consequences – positive and negative - do little to enhance learning (Marzano, 2007).**

Recognizing adherence and lack of adherence to rules and procedures requires intentional planning. Recognition and acknowledgment should be immediate. In order for this to occur, alternate proactive techniques should be utilized to monitor whether **students follow the classroom rules and procedures.**

Recognizing Adherance and Lack of Adherance to Rules and Procedures

Recognizing Adherence

- **Verbal and Nonverbal Affirmations**

  - **Verbal**—use of phrases that confirm adherence or positive behavior such as thank you, great job, that's excellent, etc. and descriptions of the commendable behavior and how it contributed positively to the class environment

  - **Nonverbal**—use of signals that a rule or procedure has been followed such as smiles, nods, high fives, thumbs-up, OK sign, etc. to acknowledge students' positive influence and credible behavior

- **Tangible Recognition**

  - Concrete recognition such as privileges, activities, or items as a reward for positive behavior (e.g., Friday Fun activities, lunch with the teacher in her room, daily recognition forms, token economies)

- **Home Recognition**

  - Recognition that extends to the student's home including phone calls, emails, texts, notes, and certificates communicating positive behavior

Recognizing Lack of Adherence

- **Verbal and Nonverbal Cues**

  - **Verbal**—comments that remind students that he or she is not following the rules or procedure at

The techniques used to recognize adherence and lack of adherence to rules and procedures should help students follow the established rules and procedures.

There are many different techniques that could be used for this purpose. *Techniques provided are a sample and should not be considered a comprehensive list.*

the moment such as "Bill, think about what you are doing right now" or "Mary, is what you are doing helping you focus your attention?"

- **Nonverbal**—use of eye contact, proximity, subtle gestures (e.g., shaking the head "no," putting finger on lips, tapping a student's desk, raised eyebrows etc.) to signal inappropriate behavior.

- **Direct Cost Consequences**

  - **Time-out**—Student is asked to go to a designated place (inside or outside of the classroom) until he or she is able to provide a concrete plan to avoid similar negative behavior and is ready to resume activities with the correct behavior.

  - **Overcorrection**—is used to adjust inappropriate behavior by overcompensating for any undesirable results which occur as a result of the misbehavior. If the behavior is destructive in nature, compensation is made by repairing what was destroyed or abused (if possible). For example, if a student has drawn on their desk, he or she would be required to clean the marks of all the desks in the classroom, not just his or her desk. Overcorrection can also be used to eliminate inappropriate automatic or insensitive behaviors, but must be administered without malicious intent.

These and more techniques can be found in *Becoming a Reflective Teacher* by Robert J. Marzano (2012) and *A Handbook for Classroom Management that Works*, by Marzano, et al (2005).

Using Engagement Strategies
When Students Are Not Engaged

Engagement is influenced by four basic needs. **Emotions** and students' levels of **interest** in the content or task impact their attention level and lead to compliant behavior and awareness. To move passed this level of compliant awareness into cognitive engagement, students must consider the content and task worthy. In other words they must consider it **important** and believe they have the ability to accomplish the task, or **self-efficacy**. These four needs highlight the students' emotions, cognition, and voice in learning and development.

The four questions students subconsciously ask themselves to determine attention and engagement are:

How do I feel?

Am I interested?

Is this important?

Can I do this?

Engagement strategies should always be intentionally planned, but overt action may be required to engage, reengage, or increase student engagement during the learning process. Various spontaneous techniques may be required to reestablish and maintain active engagement.

Five Areas or Factors that Stimulate Student Engagement	
High Energy	Utilization of physical activity, enthusiasm, intensity, and quick pacing when working with students to promote engagement and motivation
Missing Information	Capitalization on the innate human need for closure by asking students to discover and supply missing information
The Self-System	Incorporation of topics, ideas, and processes that students find appealing and valuable
Mild Pressure	Participation in activities involving questioning, games, and friendly competitions to focus on key elements of the learning process
Mild Controversy and Competition	Involvement in structured and closely managed nonthreatening debates, tournaments, and other team-based activities

Using Engagement Strategies When Students Are Not Engaged

TECHNIQUES

Planned Techniques

ACADEMIC GAMES AND INCONSEQUENTIAL COMPETITION

- **What Is the Question?**
  An activity similar to the game show 'Jeopardy!' where content information is placed in a matrix with content-based categories across the top and progressive point values and levels of difficulty down the side. Students or teams select a point value and its corresponding "content clue" then answer the clue in the form of a question. If the student or team's answer indicates understanding (is complete and correct), points are awarded and the team earns the chance to go again. If answered incorrectly or incompletely, opposing teams have an opportunity to answer and earn points. Another variation is to offer the "clue" to all teams at once and award points to all that respond correctly.

- **Which One Doesn't Belong?**
  Word groups with three or more similar terms and one that is different are created. Students work independently or in groups to pick out the term that does not belong and write down why they think it is different.

- **Classroom Feud**
  A multiple choice, fill-in-the blank, or short answer question is developed for every student in class. Students are organized into teams and take turns responding to questions. When the teacher presents a question, the "responder" has 15 seconds

The techniques used to engage students should verify active engagement in learning.

There are many different techniques that could be used for this purpose. *Techniques provided are a sample and should not be considered a comprehensive list.*

to confer with their team then answer the question. If answered correctly, a point is awarded. If not answered correctly the opposing teams get a chance to answer and earn points. When every student on all teams has functioned as a responder, the team with the most points wins the feud.

PHYSICAL MOVEMENT

- **Body Representations**
  Students briefly act out important content, terms, or critical aspects of a topic.

- **Vote With Your Feet**
  Possible responses to questions are assigned to a corner or other location in the room (e.g., true/false; incorrect, partially correct, and correct; multiple answers; alternative choice). Students move to the location in the room they believe represents the correct or best response. Students are asked to explain why they think the response they chose is correct.

LIVELY PACING

- **Parking Lot**
  To prevent from getting sidetracked, stuck, or bogged down, side issues and related questions that arise during instruction are written on a sticky note, chart paper, or the board and are revisited after everyone has had time to think and gather information about them.

- **Timely Transitions**
  Logical, decisive, and efficient transitions between activities are routinely employed to maintain effective pacing.

INTENSITY AND ENTHUSIASM

- **Personal Stories**
  Insight, appreciation, or real-world connections to the content are shared through a personal story to

make the information more accessible and help students gain a new perspective.

- **Humor**
Funny headlines, silly quotes, cartoons, amusing questions, and purposeful errors can integrate humor into the content. Only self-directed humor that is tasteful and appropriate for the audience should be employed.

FRIENDLY CONTROVERSY

- **Town Hall Meeting**
To engage students with a complex issue from multiple perspectives, students assume designated roles during a town hall meeting. Roles are based on the people or groups most likely to have a strong opinion or be affected by a new policy or issue. Students participate in an open discussion, staying in character with their respective assigned roles, and argue from that point of view while the teacher mediates. At the end of the discussion a debriefing occurs and students evaluate their own performances and the discussion as a whole.

- **Class Vote**
The merits of various positions on an issue, problem, or policy are introduced during instruction. Students are asked to choose a position and work together to further study and explore its point of view. Each group then takes turns presenting the facts, opinions, and ideas as they relate to their position on the issue. After all groups have shared and arguments have been heard, students are asked to vote. Students swayed by the final discussion may switch positions at this time. The students then reflect on the thought process that led them to their current perspective on the issue.

UNUSUAL INFORMATION

- **Guest Speakers**
  Students listen to real-world applications of the content being learned as guests share experiences from their careers.

- **Teacher-Presented Intriguing Information**
  Interesting facts or trivia related to the content are interjected into instruction to capture the attention of students.

SOCIAL AND STUDENT INTERESTS

- **Interest Surveys**
  At the beginning of the year or unit, students are asked to identify what they wish to explore or investigate regarding the content. These specific student interests and goals are then incorporated into the lessons and units of instruction.

- **Learning Profiles**
  Students are asked to complete formal or informal inventories, surveys, or discussions to determine the circumstances and conditions under which they learn best and ways they prefer to express themselves. Throughout instruction, options are provided that allow students to choose the preferred approach, format, or process to help them best learn and express themselves.

Establishing and Maintaining Effective Relationships

KEY CRITERIA

Two dynamics make up the teacher-student relationship. One is providing a sense of guidance and **control** both behaviorally and academically. The other is providing a sense of **cooperation and concern** in order for teachers and students to form a team devoted to the well-being of the classroom community.

To establish and maintain effective relationships:

- Provide academic **direction and guidance** by communicating learning targets, tracking progress, presenting feedback, and celebrating success.

- Convey **clarity of purpose** by providing intention, consistency, and reliably enforcing positive and negative consequences to strengthen the environment.

- Project a sense of **emotional objectivity** by recognizing that emotions are natural and inevitable. Monitoring thoughts and emotions, reframing student behavior in terms that are not as offensive, and maintaining a cool exterior can help communicate guidance, control, care, and concern.

- Make an effort to get to know something about each student and bring their personal interests into the content by **personalizing learning activities** to convey that you care about their interests and to make them feel part of the community of learners.

Establishing and maintaining effective relationships should always be intentionally planned. Various techniques may be required to make students feel part of the classroom community.

In *The Art and Science of Teaching* (2007), Marzano states "arguably the quality of the relationships teachers have with students is the keystone of effective management and perhaps even the entirety of teaching."

Establishing and Maintaining Effective Relationships

The techniques used to establish and maintain effective relationships with students should verify that they feel part of the classroom community.

There are many different techniques that could be used for this purpose. *Techniques provided are a sample and should not be considered a comprehensive list.*

UNDERSTANDING STUDENTS' INTERESTS AND BACKGROUNDS

- **Opinion Questionnaires**
  Opinion polls that discover student perspectives on classroom content.

- **Teacher-Student Conferences**
  One-on-one opportunities to ask probing questions to more deeply understand students' interests, perspectives, and experiences.

- **Six Word Autobiographies**
  Students write a biography in exactly six words, and the teacher leads a discussion in which students share and explain their autobiographies.

- **Quotes**
  Students collect and share quotes that describe their personalities and interests and show personal connections to the content.

DISPLAYING OBJECTIVITY AND CONTROL

- **Interpreting Communication Styles Understanding how various communication styles**
  (assertive connector, apathetic avoider, junior therapist, bulldozer, and hider) affect communication and emotional reactions to prevent from demonstrating personal offense at student behavior.

- **Active Listening and Speaking**
  To interact with students in a calm and controlled fashion, focus on what the student is saying and try to understand the student's viewpoint. Remain

neutral in body posture, gestures, and facial expressions but acknowledge the student was heard by summarizing their statement.

- **Self-Reflection**
Daily reflection about consistency when enforcing positive and negative consequences to determine if a balance between the two was obtained. If not, further reflection may be necessary on opportunities to better exhibit consistent objectivity in the future.

USING VERBAL AND NONVERBAL BEHAVIORS TO INDICATE AFFECTION

- **Scheduled Interaction**
Create a schedule to ensure regular interaction with each student by selecting a few students each day to seek out and talk to. This could be done in class, the lunchroom, between classes in the hallways, or before or after school.

- **Attend Student Functions**
Show affection and interest in students that may feel alienated by attending after-school activities in which the student is involved. Let the student know you plan to attend and try to connect with the student at the event.

- **Assign Student Roles**
To indicate affection, assign rotating roles to specific tasks in class (distributing materials, taking care of the class pet, collecting assignments)

- **Humor**
Utilize playful banter, jokes, self-directed humor incorporated into the classroom to create an enjoyable, positive learning environment. Laugh at yourself, add humorous items to assignments, initiate Joke Fridays, funny hat days, or mismatched sock days to create a warm, fun climate in the classroom.

These and more techniques can be found in *Becoming a Reflective Teacher* by Robert J. Marzano (2012).

Communicating High Expectations
for All Students

Conveying high behavioral and academic expectations drives and fortifies high student achievement. No matter the background of the student, quality work should always be anticipated and required. It is important that **value and respect be demonstrated to all students** at all times. Differential treatment between high performing and low performing students should be avoided.

An affective tone and positive emotions should be established where verbal praise and friendly nonverbal attention and responsiveness are communicated impartially. The quality of interactions with students should be of a high level and consistent. Support should be provided for all students as needed no matter their achievement level.

Appreciation for student responses should be exhibited. A **questioning culture** should be established that encourages and requires participation. Students should feel comfortable taking risks or making mistakes without fear of negative comments or disrespect from peers or the teacher.

In order to avoid differential treatment, communicating high expectations for all students should be intentionally planned. Various techniques may be utilized to ensure all **students feel the teacher has high expectations of them.**

Communicating High Expectations for All Students

TECHNIQUES

Techniques used to communicate high expectations should verify that all students feel the teacher has high expectations for them regardless of background and achievement level.

There are many different techniques that could be used for this purpose. *Techniques provided are a sample and should not be considered a comprehensive list.*

Demonstrating Value and Respect

Technique	Description
Verbal Interactions	Verbal interchanges used uniformly with all students that communicate respect and value and promote a positive classroom environment include: • Playful dialogue • Addressing students in a manner they view as respectful • Affective tone of voice • Acknowledging and expressing appreciation for involvement • Providing productive feedback
Nonverbal Interactions	Behaviors used uniformly with all students that communicate value and respect and promote a positive classroom environment without using words include: • Eye contact • Smiling • Proximity • Gestures

Asking Questions

Technique	Description
Question Levels	Ask cognitively complex questions that require students to make inferences, analyze information, evaluate conclusions, and utilize knowledge. All students should be asked rigorous questions regardless of their background or achievement level. Questions should guide students' thinking and increase their levels of processing, leading them to a deeper understanding of the content. Support should be provided as needed to those who may need help or encouragement to respond.
Expect Evidence and Support	Reinforce high expectations for all students by requiring similar levels of evidence and support for answers from every student. Every time a student makes a claim, require grounds and backing be provided. If inferences are made to answer a question, require all students explain their inferences.
Track Responses	Call on students randomly and not simply those who raise their hands. Use a class list or seating chart to indicate who answered questions or has been asked. If necessary, focus on specific students by circling their names and tracking how often they ask or respond to questions throughout the class.

Probing Incorrect Answers

Technique	Description
Layered Response Process	This process can be used by teachers or by students when working with peers. <u>Acknowledge the student's willingness and effort</u> in responding. Next, <u>emphasize what was correct and incorrect</u> in the student's response. If the answer was totally incorrect, identify the question that the incorrect response would have answered. Finally <u>provide support to help</u> the student answer correctly such as: more time to think, hints and cues, modify or restate the original question, or ask a smaller part of the original question. At times it may be appropriate to provide the correct answer and ask the student to elaborate on it, restate it in his or her own words, or provide an example.

Answer Revision	Use elaborative interrogation that encourages the student to probe his or her answer until he or she realizes that the answer is not justifiable. Use questions like the following to kindle the student's thought process: • *How do you know that to be true?* • *What evidence can you give to support this?*
Partner Query	When a student provides an incorrect answer to a question, ask *all* students to turn to a partner and reflect on the question and answer provided. Allow students to share views, discuss, and correct their thinking while working with a peer. Ask the student to restate his or her initial response after conferring with a peer. The student can then provide a revised response; quote the partner's answer, or ask the partner for assistance while replying to the question.

These and more techniques can be found in *Becoming a Reflective Teacher* by Robert J. Marzano (2012).